THE HIDDEN MODEL

THE
HIDDEN
MODEL

DAVID YEZZI

 TRIQUARTERLY BOOKS | NORTHWESTERN UNIVERSITY PRESS | EVANSTON, ILLINOIS

TriQuarterly Books
Northwestern University Press
Evanston, Illinois 60208-4210

Printed in the United States of America

10 9 8 7 6 5 4 3 2 1

ISBN 0-8101-5144-8 (cloth)
ISBN 0-8101-5145-6 (paper)

Library of Congress Cataloging-in-Publication data are available from
the Library of Congress.

The paper used in this publication meets the minimum requirements
of the American National Standard for Information Sciences—
Permanence of Paper for Printed Library Materials, ANSI Z39.48-1992.

For Sarah and Susannah,
and for my parents

There is a place that some men know,
I cannot see the whole of it
Nor how I came there.

—Allen Tate

CONTENTS

ACKNOWLEDGMENTS

I gratefully acknowledge the following publications for publishing these poems:

Columbia: "On a Mandarin Inscription"
Flâneur: "Bicoastal," "Nostalgia for a New City"
Image: A Journal of the Arts and Religion: "Foundry Road," "Vertigo in St. Paul's"
New Criterion: "Casco Passage," "Epithalamium," "On a Cliff above Seal Rocks," "What to Do with a Mountain Lake"
New England Review: "Chekhovian Landscape," "Gracie Pier," "Woman Holding a Fox"
New Republic: "Lini"
Paris Review: "Beatitudes of Poverty," "The Graven Image," "The Hidden Model," "Morandi's Bottles," "Upon Julia's Breasts"
Parnassus: "Chinese New Year," "Conversation of the Pharisees"
Pivot: "Letter to L.A."
Southwest Review: "Aporias 4–5," "Sad Is Eros, Builder of Cities"
TriQuarterly: "Allegro," "The Double," "Oracle of the Great Oak"
Verse Magazine: "Aporias 1–3," "Red Shift"
Yale Review: "Exit Pursued"

A number of these poems have been reprinted in the following:

BigCityLit: "Conversation of the Pharisees," "The Graven Image," "Woman Holding a Fox"
PN Review: "Conversation of the Pharisees"
Poetry Daily: "Epithalamium," "Exit Pursued," "Red Shift," "Woman Holding a Fox"
Salon: "Upon Julia's Breasts"

"Upon Julia's Breasts" is reprinted in *The Paris Review Book of Heartbreak, Madness, Sex, Love, Betrayal, Outsiders, Intoxication, War, Whimsy, Horrors, God,*

Death, Dinner, Baseball, Travels, the Art of Writing, and Everything Else in the World since 1953 (Picador, 2003).

A portion of this manuscript was printed by Michael Peich in a limited edition under the title *Sad Is Eros* (Aralia Press, 2003).

Many thanks to those friends and associates from whom I have received guidance and support: Neil Azevedo, Susan Betz, Lucie Brock-Broido, Alfred Corn, Jim Dembowski, Ben Downing, John Foy, Dana Gioia, Susan Hahn, Roger Kimball, Hilton Kramer, Daniel Kunitz, Herbert Leibowitz, Robert Messenger, Michael Peich, and C. Dale Young. I am grateful to Stanford University for a Wallace Stegner Fellowship in poetry, which allowed me to complete much of this book, and to my teachers and colleagues at Stanford: Eavan Boland, W. S. Di Piero, Kenneth Fields, Joannie Makowski, Christian Wiman, Brett Foster, Monica Youn, Andrew Feld, and Rick Barot.

THE HIDDEN MODEL

ONE

BEATITUDES OF POVERTY

No single excess, nothing jerry-built
or squandered in a fit of thriftlessness,
accounts for what we've ended with. Despite

our frugal care, the stores are sapped; red ink
replaces black. The sideboard's single fig
bites off a taunt; tea steeps from last week's bag.

Now rash displays of force are the domain
of every man persuasive in his loss,
whether forfeiture of property or just

the planned disintegration of a trust.
Ah, my dear, this blessed turnabout
has laid us open to a bitter faith.

Blessed are the keepers of contempt,
and blessed all the fallow acreage
left still unworked. We cherish our reward.

Our giving in embodies the reverse
by which we gain this holy poverty
and, with each vicissitude, a certain grace.

MORANDI'S BOTTLES

His slender Moselles would, in truth, describe
the scumbled shapes of autumn, color leached
as from a cheek, sallow, opaque; or five
green Burgundies might best contrive to teach
suave consolations of the midday sun,
despite what light his studio could hold;
for deeper shades of solitude he'd run
the throat of a Chianti, inked in bold,
netting with his crosshatch all he saw
suggested—ruined cityscapes, stone pines,
the shape a shoulder makes, or nature pausing—
that the mundane might offer with its lines
what sighs beneath the surface, even there,
of the unillumined world where it comes clear.

WOMAN HOLDING A FOX

Buried inside, page 3, below the fold,
a woman crumpled on fresh dirt begins to get the gist:
that she has lost the use of her left leg, that when she tripped
          her hip gave out. Shock explains
this all to her, a self-assured young doctor mouthing, *Rest.*

The reason for the break, a rabid fox
that came at her when she stepped out for half a cigarette.
Age seventy-nine, the paper said; she hadn't toppled far,
          merely down her few front steps,
but late enough that no one finds her till the following day.

And here's the eerie part. Just when she thinks
to drag herself down to the curb, the twisted fox comes back.
In hours her arms are bitten blue, waving her one defense.
          Her glasses lost in tufted grass,
she hears it thread the underbrush before she sees it leap.

At two o'clock, a nurse toggles the lamp.
Something for the pain. Since after dark, the fox has come
to look on her as prey, the way he circles and descends.
          This is no dream, she tells herself.
Yet it had seemed unreal from the initial streak of red:

a comedy at first, a photo-op,
then something else, an eye-white flash our unsuspecting trust
shields us from until the outward show no longer jibes.

She's landed in her garden row,
her Marlboro still smoking on the carefully weeded path.

Beyond the gate a sunset has begun,
the swatch of sky above her roof dyed jacaranda-blue.
These are things she sees as she assumes things can't get worse.
But then they do. When it returns,
she clasps it to herself. Somehow she's managed to affix

small hands around its muzzle and bared teeth.
All night she feels it panting and enraged, then weirdly calm.
So off and on for hours until someone spots her there.
A neighbor comes, she knows that now.
But on the sedge she hadn't guessed that it would end so well.

As for what crowds her head: a single thought
repeated in contrition, while the same minute extends,
infinitely regressing between mirrors set opposed.
Music's playing down the hall,
carried on a crack of light that shows the door ajar.

It's nearly dawn. I have not killed the fox,
my arms barely keep him hemmed, my fingers have gone limp.
Across the lawn an amniotic slick of dew gives off
a silver sheen and sudden cold.
I'm glad you happened by, she wryly croaks when he appears.

Before he batters in the hissing fox,
he asks her why she simply didn't let it run away.
I know this creature pretty well by now. She shows her skin.
It's true, she understands the fox
and wonders if she hasn't always known that he was there,

known it when her first child was born,
and known it, too, the day her husband died three years ago.
At any rate she knows it now, will always keep him close
        in her embrace from day to day,
up to a time when memories of these no longer serve.

CHINESE NEW YEAR

Confetti in the streets
coagulates like spoors of dragon's blood,
running gold and purple underfoot,
as the horse-year stumbles beneath the ram-year
and fire spills from children's hands.
We've come too late to see

the pageant go. This codicil
of scraps, of gaping faces glowing past,
points away from celebration, back
toward street-ruin and spiking temperatures,
as the old year slackens and rasps.
Downstairs, we take a corner

in your usual noodle shop.
Tables are manic now with revelers
sluicing tea. Lazy Susans grind.
Bowls of duck and shredded pork perform
in a theater of plenty, while,
streetside, crowds plod north.

And like all those who come back
from the dead, you are a day-lit phantom,
somnambulant, with twitching hands and dust
caked in livid hair. I'm glad you lived,
that you scraped through when thousands died
and war rooted in frozen earth.

I tell you how in dreams
I watch an acrid fire-cloud consume
the sky-high island, covering the park
and leaving nothing breathing after it.
    And you, who saw such things for real,
        no longer dream, you say.

    Outside, I buy a dragon
for my daughter, just turned one. Its eyes are jewels
of plastic gold set in papier-mâché
and bordered with a feather-boa mane.
    She understands nothing of dragonkind—
        the ones that mark the year

    with undulating scales and mirth,
and those that come by night, coiling around
some nameless prey, darkening her sight
in soot. And will it quiet her, sweet girl,
    to hear it's gone, just shadow-play, like smoke,
        from fires hissing out?

CHEKHOVIAN LANDSCAPE

Yelping beneath a lilac bush,
his dogs have rooted out the hind parts of a deer,
and he has slipped in noiselessly among sumac,
      bloodred this time of year
      against a sky like smoke,
         to where in slush
      the body lies damasked and dismembered.
      He remembers

he must find the road by dark,
and so he pauses only briefly now to wonder
how the mangled creature might have come to this—
      or he, for that matter,
      how has he come to this?
         Tracing an arc,
      he walks a line of elms back toward the lake.
         Wolves will take

a buck apart down to the bone,
gracefully, he thinks, much as a watch's hand
swipes an hour away with brute efficiency.
      Their pack reclaims the land.
      Just past some blackened trees,
         he turns for home
in time to see a single goshawk going.
         It's started to snow.

The bird ascends the gray, a sign
of something imminent, though what he cannot tell.
Trying out a knack for prophecy, he feels
  he's staring in a well,
   yet that darkness will not yield
    its obscured lines
  to him. So, though he watches after it,
   the hawk stays mute.

Twilight sifts down to dusk, then night,
as portents and what they point to disappear behind
a veil of heavy flakes. They have absorbed both sound
  and light. He cannot find
  the trail back into town.
   His dogs act lost.
He stumbles, imagines someone else's life,
   his own, his wife's.

She's waited up for me, he tells
himself. It took him time to learn to disappoint her,
and she's less patient now. Grown dizzy in the white,
  all distinctions blurred
  of sky and land, he fights
   to see it still:
the beacon of his windows' oil fires
   through the freeze.

EXIT PURSUED

Sometimes she almost smells night-blooming jasmine,
humid above the plywood balustrade.
      Cue horse and carriage-bells,
      which in the house combine
with piped-in wind to mock the pact they'd made,
she and her lover. He heaves the gate again,
        slides out in rain.
Tonight again she feels a falling spell.

And half an hour from now a pistol shot
will end what hopes she'd had to save her son
      from injuring himself.
      Offstage, the scene is not
so ripe with fate: tea steeps for Scotch, the gun's
a carousel of starter's blanks, and blood
       pours food-dye red.
Out front, she lifts a bottle from the shelf,

half fills a glass with sherry, and begins
to argue with the local curate on
      her failure of belief.
      "Would you call it a sin,"
she rounds on him, "for me to help my son?
Or does God wish it that every son should die?"
       She's started crying.
Among her growing list of cares, a brief

pang from nowhere: Did I forget to pay
the phone this month? A week and this will all

be struck. It's dead tonight.
	Why did I take this play?
This bodice makes my chest look way too small.
Next scene, she tries her best to block these thoughts:
		"Son, have I taught
you anything that you can use to fight

the darkness when it works to draw you in?"
At intermission, she wishes she could sleep.
		Already, she can hear
		the canned music beginning.
In the accounting of her makeup lamp,
her eyes reflect the eyes of Mrs. X.
		Herself again, she takes
a snap of her own boy down from the mirror,

recognizing something in that smile
as hers. He lives twelve hours away by car,
		the years of his absence
		in that second more real
than the sleights of hand designed to bolster her:
dry cakes of powder and a brunette fall.
		She's told the call—
five minutes, please. Some offstage violence,

one scene of grieving, then she can return
to her bed with the guy who plays her son.
		She loves a sure thing, knowing
		how it will end: the burn
of whiskey and the letting go. *What's done
cannot be undone,* she's so often said.
		She clears her head
and enters left just as her child's going.

APORIAS

i

What more assurance than these cobbled walks—
one paving stone abutting on a next,
that next foretelling a farther cracked expanse,
and each intrinsically allied to meet
the mindless footfalls of the passerby—
could we need of continuum? Or what
firmer proof the days dovetail this way
than that one street follows-on another street;
curb gives way to bridge; suburb, to mere,
cementing our assumptions in a thought,
as the tightrope walker learns to trust the wire,
yet who, midact, suspends his step to wonder
just how it is he's come this way, or that
such bedrock certainties have led him here?

ii

As with a grain of pearl-provoking grit
or a burn the tongue returns to, the mistake
sneaks in as irritation first—an ache
we learn to live with, then come to expect,
and may even grow desirous of in time;
though, when metastasized, grown absolute,
it gleams as rainbow nacre gleams, a brute
fact, a semiprecious paradigm
of our lustrous and perfect falling down;

so that as the act assumes new worth and weight,
it makes a gloss of faults that came before,
taking on, layer by layer, a second skin
to outshine the common earth that bodied it,
a prized transgression of the first water.

iii

A clutch of asters in a stoneware vase,
its bright titanium mottled with moth-wing,
atrophies—a satire on former thriving:
leaves' quick familiarity with the air's
harsher elements, the tempered *snick*
of rootlessness, arrangement, and decay.
Still life or *nature morte?* The ocher play
of shade and sunlight illustrates a trick
upon the eye, the commonplace as paradox,
where each framed moment is life still, and yet
a ghost of its decline, a gesture sketch
to trace the thing that's missed; such brushwork makes
our reclaiming and relinquishing the same,
a cenotaph, the utterance of a name.

iv

Along the Hudson, fog dissolves our sight,
like sugar broken up in lukewarm tea.
All month, a heat wave holds, from airless nights
subsiding, in the damp expectancy
of rain, to morning skies weakly infused
with what has not yet gathered force to fall.
At white on white, the eye becomes confused.
The grains a solvent will not hold we call

precipitate, and buildings are the forms
these crystals take, assembled from the haze,
a craggy foreground for the promised storm.
Sluggish as a coming mood, for days
the front bogs down, though, always when it breaks,
it takes the form of grace that violence takes.

      v

Ivory beneath a wind-whipped swell of bays,
a peony has flowered overnight,
insinuated as a cutting phrase,
until its petals, countless shades of white,
erupted in a riot of pure scent.
With one suggestion from its hidden root,
like Cassio's stitched handkerchief, it went
from scoffed-at rumor to the very proof
waved as a taunt through humid seaside air.
Before you spoke, I barely noticed it,
but I've since cut it down and placed it where
it's never far from mind, so that I sit
admiring, much as you would have me do,
how bright and fated things look when they bloom.

THE HIDDEN MODEL

A PENTIMENTO

What vague dispassion or crisis of hope
entered the artist's head when, leaving off
his study of a woman, he began,

still on the same stretcher, another work—
this one, too, the portrait of a girl
but with, restorers tell us, different eyes

and gown, an altogether different grin?
His reused canvas (probably prescribed
by a lack of means) was not unusual,

though certainly there'd been a loss of paint:
umbers crowded at their vanishing,
or his crisp siennas fixed as auburn hair.

What care he took to cover them, beginning
so nearly with the features of the old,
obliterating, reshaping a cheek,

or caressing the neck another way,
till slowly, finally, he would repent
the promise in the former figure there.

Beyond the gossip of historians,
nothing of his first model is known,
nothing, that is, the naked eye can hold

as proof her smaller hands had come before.
Still, some shadings of the face persist,
a capsule of that day that she'd been glad

to sit a second hour by him, posing.
Had he known outright he'd never finish it?
Perhaps just this: that such work's never lost,

that what eluded each false start might serve
to save his latest version, the crisis turned
by a surer hand, rehearsing what was missed.

TWO

LINI

i

Through live oaks, sunset's sanguine oval slips its limits, grows
cold, oblate, until thin, receding, near gone, merely blue.

ii

Blight over. The dog rolls into a farther sky. Its loss
costs no more than what we give for this augury of ice.

iii

Corn low, a new moon with the old still in its arms, stores full,
wool piled for mending: it's now the well blessed begin to mourn.

CONVERSATION OF THE PHARISEES

AFTER REMBRANDT'S *HUNDRED GUILDER PRINT*

Such upright citizens, all honest Joes,
      these legal men sketched in at left
so sparingly they almost blanch from view;
          how they huddle,
        dull to radiance

and fouled in the lines affixing them,
      oblivious to Christ's light caught
across their faces, like a harrowing
          of their tight circle,
        as they natter on.

A few, you say, acknowledge Him and turn
      intently or with skepticism
intact—still, they have understood more than
          their purblind fellows,
        who, while arguing

arcana of Scripture with which to test
      the man, have left off noticing
what even children and the sick see plainly.
          And we are quick
        to read the gulf between

ourselves and those gray priests in antique hats
      (aligned instead with the heroes),
and wise to the fact of their ignorance,
        though we, like them,
      have missed the central point:

that they are there for us, to represent
      those from whom the truth's been held,
the more bemused, who lord the blameless life,
        its sureties,
      over the fallen ones.

We, too, have mastered certainties, taken solace
      in precision, keeping dates,
and the long code of standard practices
        like compositions
      bitten into brass,

while laws we've missed, or lapsed in looking for,
      remain of necessity
unremarkable and always close,
        so many motes
      adrift in dark corners.

THE GRAVEN IMAGE

Hundreds of people stood . . . in the courtyard
of a Post Avenue apartment building to see . . .
whether a bathroom window shimmered with the
image of Jesus Christ or was just smudged.
                                    —*New York Observer*

Not that anyone made it, necessarily,
inlaid with enamel, cast in gold;
not painted like an ornament

or candlelit behind an altar screen.
It surfaced in the most mundane of spots,
at an ordinary hour, squibs of light

fracturing the unlikely vessel,
a window—not stained or even leaded—
just a pane of unimportant glass.

Simply appeared (who knows how many weeks
it went unnoticed? was it always so?):
the all-familiar image of the Christ—

longhaired, bearded like on the Turin shroud—
reflecting on the crowd that heard and came,
doubtless, to divine the glory there.

And they had known him. Perhaps it matched
the drawings in some illustrated text,
the pictures children seldom get beyond

in their barely hirsute search for holiness
(*I* was one of those). Or was it nearer
to the revelation witnessed on the road,

when nothing like himself, in foreign clothes,
he showed himself to several of his flock?
"Some people need a sign," the pastor said—

the inward search replaced by outward show—
as, overhead, high clouds betrayed the forms
of a whiskered face, an anvil, mountain, cow.

VERTIGO IN ST. PAUL'S

Circled in the guide,
the portals of empyrean:
views from St. Thomas's Tower or the spatter
of lamp-lit London, its gilding hurled against
the canvases a rainy night prepares.

Seen from a rooftop bar,
taxis orbit in darkness,
shuddering past the Marble Arch. Up here,
escorts in strapless dresses smoke, their nearness
to me dawning like straight Scotch. How well

their calm disturbs my own.
A flash from hours before:
me crumpled on the steps of St. Paul's dome,
grasping at the rail, and spider-crawling,
supine, slowly, step-by-step to ground.

Just then a kid in flipflops
clacked down the spiral steps,
condoling when I pointed up. He passed.
Earthbound, I looked to heaven one last time,
at the roof and at the stairs in space,

relinquishing all that,
unable to grapple higher,
though children do it easily every day.
Now more than sights I saw, I want that view,
fallen and sick the more I thought to climb.

HAND TO MOUTH

"How much is enough?" she snorted, gamely
twisting a sprig of watercress in the air,
then straining its jade leaves through her bright teeth,
and I thought of some friends we knew in Brooklyn—
he a painter, she a perfect 4
who made her money as a mannequin,
a fit-model on Seventh Avenue.
Childless, they kept a German shepherd bitch
who managed better on beef bones and lettuce
than they on what they ate most days. Each month,
they'd lug another sack of kibble home,
and for themselves brown rice in five-pound bags.

The dog died; they survived, as it turned out.
(He wolfed a ball of cord that gave his guts
a snarl the hospital could not cut loose.
Hand-tied, they put him down.) Last we heard,
the two had gone to Greece and thrown themselves
upon the kindness of an island village,
where he became a goatherd, work that paid
for food enough. For shelter, they relied
on balmy weather, lean-tos, and cleared ground.
No recent news has made it back, except
that they've become a nuisance in the town.
And though the snow's arrived there, they're still gone.

So we lose touch, like with the newlyweds
who sold our wedding gifts and moved out West.

We hadn't missed them much, till common friends
reported recently the two have split.
He's lost his mind again (believes he's Christ)
and disappeared more fully than the friends
we keep as enemies, whom we still prize,
since secretly we can't abide a world
that they're not in, so rather than put them
completely out of mind we hold them close
and scorn them, as they do us, with the same
shared venom, although once we called it love.

How different are the friendships that endure:
inviolate, well founded, decorous,
though never seared by that eruptive heat
that harms the people closest to our hearts.
And so we keep the things we never had.
The blithe acquaintances we hardly mind—
those who take our calls, or meet for lunch,
commiserate (we'd do the same for them)—
have let us know that, while we are not loved,
we are well liked. Just so, the opposite:
it's those we have that we will surely lose,
those focal points that show the world slip by.

Across the oaken restaurant, a woman
has reddened into tears, and we're at pains
to know if she's just broken with the guy
who slides his chair and walks to comfort her.
A stiff embrace broadcasts their rapprochement
to other furtive onlookers like us
who trust that they have made it up for now,
although their rift might open up the same
tomorrow night, or some night in the span

allotted them from their communal time
in this city and while they both are young
and getting by (or not) on God knows what.

FOUNDRY ROAD

i

Once a banded slough, no trace remains
of the discarded road—two wagon tracks
dipped to the water table of wet clay

beside a brooklet—where the blacksmith's boy
had sunk his spokes so deep they stuck
and dragged old boards to ease his team across.

Sumacs crowd the field where the workshop stood
that housed the forge. Their conical reds
retain a furnace-glow against the pounded

sheets of sky, gray in lightly falling snow.
Driving by, we break the plod of seasons,
the workaday strain of forearms, raw

from firing iron or shoveling coal
that the bellows had inspired to burn white-hot,
approaching less the footpace over shale

of the mile-walk home from the foundry at dusk,
than the forward roll of history's *whoosh*
glimpsed as a blur in the driver's-side glass.

Bound in this accretion of soggy hills
are the losses, too, of one winter afternoon:
light and heat spend early.

We return from the frail hours of watching
coffinside, exhausted by our prayers
and the ruined eyes of aunts we hardly know.

My blue suit doesn't fit me anymore—
how right, since I am awkward with my pain—
and you, who have his name and were born

on his birthday, are the brother I never see
except on mischance days like these
when the family is wrenched together again

to press our thumbs in how we've come to share
the common fiber woven to remember
what binds us, what is grounded to this land,

and what is left to shield us as the seasons
whorl our features from this place, like the pebbles
worn from stones, like a scattering of ash.

iii
Not far from here, behind white lilac trees,
there is a spot so filled with redolence
that as a boy I'd dream of flying over it.

Climbing through twigs and leaves
till free of the treetops where they'd graze
my naked legs, I'd feel the fear of falling

like a weight pressing on my lungs
or a stone from which the heat's been drained
radiating cold in the cavity of my heart.

But always—it came by breathing in—
the ground would swell beneath me as I fell
only a bit too fast so that my head rang

when it hit the muddy knoll. Today, as then,
no flight seems possible, only falling,
heavy with the memories already cooling

like metal hissing in a trough
of what's too difficult to keep in mind,
which, if memory were meant, might keep its burn.

WHAT TO DO WITH A MOUNTAIN LAKE

We pushed off from the crumbled dam
      into a lake of clouds,
with duckweed plastering our chins,
      gliding without sound.

The jinking trees grew quietest
      where water sketched in the shore,
their disheveled branches wreathed
      around the mirrored air.

Three concentric circles, then,
      existed there at once;
widest was the wilderness,
      the smallest one our own.

But what was that unruined stillness
      of the lucid middle ring,
which from inside the world of flaws
      bridged us with everything?

Water colder than the wind,
      so green and darkly clear
that looking downward into it
      we saw just where we were:

one swimmer floating near the other
      above a mottled sky
reflected in that seamless span
      supporting you and me.

THREE

SAD IS EROS, BUILDER OF CITIES

A WRECKING SITE, LOWER EAST SIDE

Leveled to a ruin of cinder block,
the walls and gimcrack shards of tenement
make a more enduring bid for order:

No further demolition will undo
this present lack, no bright ascendancy
seduce its will or struggle to climb back.

It marks a certain beauty, a blank snow
hugging the swaddled torso of the ground
in mended white, a uniform, a gown.

Draped piecemeal in a length of bridal cloth,
the sky meets its reflection, tinted dun
with the pallor of this lacuna's crumbled stone.

Perhaps the planners have already drawn
fresh blueprints for another building here,
yet something of the place itself resists

such strivers' fragile meddling and scolds
the futility of each attempt torn down—
if no time soon, still, someday: do not build.

ALLEGRO

We're friends,
or were.
The end's
obscure:

a dis-
connect,
or did our
neglect . . . ?

No matter.
It's off—
muffle
the cough

of sorrow
with a glove.
Or was it
love?

Ovid
fishes,
but Caesar's
wishes

will not be
reversed.

And we're
far worse

than they
at patronage
and praise.
That age

is gone,
like every
kindness
we

cashiered.
In the end,
not to
depend

on me
has done
you good.
You've won.

Who thrives,
prevails.
No contact
through the mails,

no telephone.
For the rest,
you are
blessed

no longer
to lie
(or hardly).
So am I.

ON A CLIFF ABOVE SEAL ROCKS

Behind us the city, the ocean below us.
Cold wind combed the headlands; your fingers were cold.

How long the light lasted there, light that at nightfall
moved over the transom of a slow-moving yawl.

We kept its sails in sight, our sight closing in
until, just then, the sun was under. Or then?

Or had I missed the instant, the instant *exactly,*
when evening crossed into night, when the sea

darkened, becoming as dark as the land had?
It had been like the first trace of joy when we had it,

which now seems so perfect but, then, seemed like now—
low and quotidian, difficult; difficult, low.

ON A MANDARIN INSCRIPTION

I have no Chinese; yet how these calligraphs
do articulate the spattered flight of swans,
or pines tortured by sleet on mountain paths.
Here, beside this columned hand, along a pond,
an introspective couple walks in clothes
blazoned with ceremony. Maybe a bride
and groom? Are these words for them? Who knows?
Pausing for a moment, we have tried
to fathom their lovers' language, what was meant
by these . . . wishes, perhaps, written for their sake?
We come up empty, foiled by the foreign script;
though such kindnesses, even in one's native talk,
are as indecipherable—mute acts of faith
in what we've tried by fits and starts and can't sustain.

EPITHALAMIUM

FOR BEN AND MICHELE

If we, who have gleaned from towns jutting through fog
    how clarity comes in season by season,
revisit the places we've been happy, then this
    will be one. Already, we imagine, you're away,
twisted in foreign linen, recalling our faces, oval-lit,
    flushed, unglued from so much wine.
Even as the sleep you've put off past midnight works in
    like footfalls at your streetside window,
there's time for one last thought: that tomorrow holds
    another day like this. The sun-spanked piazza,
with its chugging fountain and stairs astride the canal,
    will press you in afternoon heat until dinner,
then bed.
        Over the terracing earth, our common friends
    eat, or furl curtains at an old-city casement,
or scatter for mountain finches a handful of seed.
    One threads an alley in a crosstown taxi
to a lover, while another sits leafing the elder Disraeli
    in a dog-eared edition, or tucks a blanket
round the ears of a child who woke shrieking in darkness
    from a dream of lost home. It's for us,
as for yourselves, you do this thing. Beyond tonight, we,
    who have seen in you, both singly and together,
a perfection, know nothing again may be wholly gainsaid.

And if the fealty of one for the other
constitutes a rival good to God's, then it is a balm
    He has allowed the solitary.
                                The gypsy
confides: so much of what lies ahead hides from us,
    as you estimate which she has more of,
gatti or teeth. Of course, she's right about mystery.
    So for what you knew before, you pay her,
and know it a second time, more fully now. *Ask your question*
    in two-times-twenty years, Signore. Ask her.
She will take your hand, and, still your bride, tell you
    something of why you strayed in company . . .
with children, cronies, two furballs; parents gone.
    Like a scintilla discharged from flints,
what catches the eye at night becomes the memory you keep;
    just so, the outshoots of our lives become our lives.

SUPERSTITION

FOR SHS

Lately prone to ritual,
I try these strange observances
to stay the unseen world, the pull
the lunatic admits as his:

every knuckle-bark on wood
or circumambulated ladder
helps to ease the reddened tide
of doubt drowning what's come to matter;

for not until I held a thing
that, losing, would unsettle me
or lend fortuity its sting

should our luck run less constantly
did I resort to safeguarding
the time with homespun remedy.

LETTER TO L.A.

FOR KATIE

Finally, past sunset, I begin
This note I had intended to have finished
When sleep outstripped me in a patch of light
So warming, filled with such *Gemütlichkeit,*
That I lost track of all my shoulds and oughts.
But as the sun is with you so my thoughts
Reach westward, touching down in your Pacific,
Though with pyrotechnic riffs less beatific
Than the coruscating fireworks of your bays
At evening. Sister, how are you these days?
I hope my last letter found you well.
That man you spoke of still in tow? Please tell
Him for me that he'd better muddle through
Where you're concerned, or, if he's bad to you,
He can expect an acid line from me.
(Ah, the dwindled powers of poetry!)
With regard to love, I've little else to offer:
In matters amorous let's say I suffer
From a winnowed readership, output is sparse,
And, therefore, you'll forgive me if I nurse
A few played-out clichés by way of guidance.
I find that the Old Masters are less strident
On the subject, K., than I can be. Or would.
    For nascent romance Rilke's pretty good,

Though that business on solitude's effete.
To guard another's "time apart" sounds right
But guard it too well and you might discover
Yourself alone, the other with another.
Case in point: a woman I'd been seeing
Had me cantering in circles; seems her "being"—
That's what she called it—fell in jeopardy
When pressed by what she deemed excess of *me*.
So, heeding Rainer's dictum, I drew back.
Now if I see her by a sidewalk rack
Of books down at the Strand, or crossing a street
Against the light with marked intent to squeak
By unnoticed, I feel that we're in touch.
Give distance sparely; don't give overmuch.
    Odi et amo underscores the crux.
Often, Catullus gleaned, the wandering rocks
We navigate between rise in ourselves,
The clear way to the fleece razored with shelves
Of keel-rending reef. As with the *Argo*,
The dove charting our passage takes us far, though
Not unscathed, some pinions may get sheared.
Have patience if my diatribe has veered
To tangents; one must sneak up on the truth
(I mention this in deference to your youth):
When choosing a partner, sometimes the best man's
Not one you love, but one that you can stand.
Although with me, the opposite holds sway;
My natural diffidence flips the equation
From a seller's to a buyer's marketplace;
I respect the ones who don't blanch at my face.
    Milton displays some clarity. You've read
His thoughts on marriage and the marriage bed?

They calibrate the weaknesses of man
With startling precision. If you can,
He says, avoid the winding snares of lust,
Then best abstain; or, if you feel you must
Indulge your passions, marriage holds a use
In avoiding darker shades of self-abuse.
So far, he's merely quoting old Saint Paul:
"It's better to marry than burn" (in hell?).
M.'s *Discipline* breaks its doctrinal course
When he cracks open the issue of divorce.
Here he really cooks: Why stay bound up
When incompatibility disrupts
Connubial attachment? Better to sever
Than feel trapped by a faulty bond forever.
How right that bit. In fact, he might go on.
Why stop at divorce? A good antiphon
To rehearse in response to those who force
Themselves on you is "No." A stern address
Cuts through unwanted awkwardness, and ends
The hopes of fools who fancy themselves friends.
Without exception this is what *I* do,
And that accounts for why I have so few.

    Enough. My best intentions fall to drivel
And laying bare the contents of my navel,
Where, if truth be told, resides the source
For much of my more introspective verse.
Excuse my feigned insouciance if I refuse
To ask after the weather. From the news,
I get the gist. The itch that needs a scratch
Is how Laguna Beach remains attached
To land in light of all it's undergone
From mudslides, burning, quaking; what went wrong?

Or, more important, what fresh plague comes next?
Californians must feel somehow vexed—
And that unduly—by the demiurge.
Hard not to view disaster as a scourge
When new catastrophe compounds the one
Still trailing off. Don't hesitate to phone
Whenever you can wrest a moment free
from the hurly-burly. As you think of me—
Or, if you do—know that my constant care
Is only for your happiness. Please bear
In mind my gentle cautions and dispose
Of any useless passages. I close,

                    Your Brother

UPON JULIA'S BREASTS

> Who now reads Herrick?
> —Allen Tate

Since our proscriptive age cannot abide
the mannish gazing that's objectified
the female shape (both gamine slim and more
curvaceous in its lineaments), I swore
correctness, chiefly to avoid the din
one risks to laud the callipygian.

So, turning chicken, now I praise your skin
rubbed with fresh herbs; and hungrily begin
to taste the parts you help me to prepare,
so plump, for my delight; and, ravished, dare
to broadcast that your white meat drives me wild,
dear circummortal chef, sweet Julia Child.

FOUR

BICOASTAL

i

Token of separation. Tower-proud.
Lozenge. Island. City in distress.
You fit us perfectly like tesserae
into your walled, mosaic-lined iconoclasm,
your rat tunnels and bud-strewn walks in spring.
Tectonic plate of wet streets sliding toward
repose. Toenail. Scab. Bright chandelier
and storefront sinecure. If I have left you
to the river's constant sweep, remember
that tug is fast but tidal. Axis. True north.
Recurring dream of someone come to warn.
Oubliette. *Exsilium*. Home.

ii

A sun departing west. "For hours the light's
like this," I tell you. I have observed it,
a swab grown in a petri dish, glow red,
then go. Sea: a lead-pipe horizontal.
Reefless sluiceway to reasonless night.
Lotus. Bank of succulents in bloom.
Paramour and secret temple of the telephone.
Into your shapely hands I commit all
my forgetting. When I have finished knowing you
it will be too late to take things back.
I'll drop some marker at your door and leave.
Some maimed thing. Maw. Shivered tor.

CASCO PASSAGE

I.M. PAUL WOOD, D. 1999

By midday, gouts of fog
    sock in until
we almost think the weather means some harm,
the way it runs over the harbor. Gauzy,
    a trawler on its mooring
    sputters close to home.
      A level calm.
Seams smoothed, the clouded archway shadowless:
our view lacks eye-holds, like the papered set
    of a photo shoot, merely
      figure and ground.

This morning, as we slept,
    his boat was found
grinding in circles somewhere up the reach.
A fisherman came on it stymied there,
    recrossing in the spume
    of its own wake, its wheelhouse
      ghostly, its course
a ring by Titian charcoaled in the sea.
We knew his name. And when it made the news
    the dust of pickups rose
      to clog the road:

men set out dragging rigs
    that yesterday
had yanked up heavy, bruised with mussel shells,
Phoenician purples clustered in a fist.
    Today, they're hoisted limp—
    a heartache and relief.
    One snarled clue:
some fouled line sliced from the sinking trap.
Had it jerked him in a whip-crack overboard,
    his strength sapped as he flailed
    to loose his boat?

    Now shoals of mackerel lash
    in running shallows,
each silver leap skyward through glass survived.
Down on the point, a few last headlights glare,
    then swing wide, then go.
    I have come to the water
    to clean a pail,
while you close out the damp in half-lit rooms.
A year ago, we married near this spot,
    where three white-pine trees stare
    over the bay.

    All week, his wife can watch
    hope's half-life split
daily until the hour she knows he's gone.
But for now: she looks on as he swims
    ashore—"He's strong, you know?"—
    chokes breath on sand. . . . *No sign.*
    Word goes round,

as stories of near misses start in town:
"Remember in the south, that killing gale?
    After the second night,
        with the helm

    an icy sledgehammer
        whanging my ribs,
I leaned down to your mother, who for days
could not look at the waves as high as roofs.
    'We'll die out here,' I told her,
    letting the tiller go;
        'I'm so damn tired. . . .'
The wind was through with us two hours later.
Half sunk, we made land under perfect skies,
    boys out hauling nets
        struck by the sun."

RED SHIFT

What had seemed till recently as clear as day
darkens now, beaten to violet breakers,

whose troughs' deep indigos amaze all hands,
befogging, separatist as ampersands

or the dotted line land divides along.
No bearings in this blue, no channel gong

to hark us back from our wrong turn, no scenes
of harbor, of islands wood-smoked and greening.

Still, in light of all that we've remarked
of sudden weather and the yellow stars,

best to batten down, stand watch for signs
of orange at evening, or a slackening in the lines,

trusting that this time of red alert might ease
its frequency, back in pacific seas.

HIS BOAT

KENICHI HORIE, OSAKA TO SAN FRANCISCO, 1962

    i

No bigger than a bier in a cortege and, washed with spindrift, fragile
        as a cell,
its sheets a set of fraying flagella, conduits of impulse, in a swell

that jettisons his membranous new shell across an all-engulfing field
        of spume.
A high wave hits his sloop the way a dose of topical solution hits a
        wound

scrubbed out with gauze but missing the escape from pain that fol-
        lows with the cold. No bays
or inlets, nothing that his eye can differentiate in early morning haze.

    ii

Archilochus's hedgehog, the tin sea, knows one big thing. And now
        he knows it, too.
But setting out, he'd thought more like the fox; so many things to
        keep in mind: the food,

a hundred days' worth, stowed beside some tools and extra sails; a
        box with many books;
his passport good only for Okinawa. The first night from Osaka, he
        had looked

along the shipping lanes for shadow-craft, which miles from shore
        appear as starless holes
but are freighters heading for the China Sea, Bo Hai, Tokyo, the
        Tartar Straits, and Seoul.

From breaking the horizon line to breaking through his boat is fif-
        teen minutes. So,
he sleeps for ten, then climbs on deck to smooth the gathered water
        with his eyes. Below,

he sleeps ten more: thus on and off till dawn—that is if nothing
        comes. And nothing does,
at least not yet. Though two months out, along the thirty-seventh
        parallel, he was

watching a battalion of dense rain charge with its banners over oily
        seas
when it appeared to windward, a mirage. *(It's no mirage.)* A tanker.
        When he sees

the mountain of it bearing down on him, already it's too late.
        Despite his hails,
it grinds by without slowing, its thick tail of water fanning out in sil-
        ver scales.

    iii
His mother thumbs the note he left once more and tries to keep
        from glancing toward the bay
or asking if he'll possibly turn back and put in safe at home. How
        many days

will she continue watching? From Honshu to California is five thou-
        sand miles.
No word in June, then no word in July, and he had left in May. A
        young boy smiles

at her bedside. There will never come a day when she forgets to ask if
        he'll be found.
He had planned to make it up to her, but realizes now that there's
        no sound

to adequately harbor his remorse or give her back the one thing that
        he took—
her nerves fire for a limb no longer there. He stubs the thought out,
        opening a book:

It's nice to read the news that our spring rain has visited your town.
        And this one, known
by heart: *Above the tides of leaves that drown the earth, a mountain*
        stands aloft, alone.

    iv
From its case, Kenichi lifts a sextant, letting his father weigh it in his
        hands.
He shows him how the mirrors help enlarge the arc of the perspec-
        tive; then he stands

aside to let him try. A sudden breeze. Without a pause, his father sets
        it down,
the act gone unremarked on, though Kenichi thinks of it the night
        he's almost drowned.

v

Sextants aren't much good without the sun. For three full days, a
        gale rubs out the sky;
for three nights, he steers eastward with no stars, until the wind con-
        vinces him he'll die.

The memory of it surfaces in mind the day he smells the pitchy musk
        of land.
Before the shore bobs up across the bow, damp air describes a euca-
        lyptus stand,

as flow tide sucks him toward the Golden Gate. The city, scaling
        hills, appears on fire,
its countless windows shivering the light like sextant mirrors. Stalled
        aloft, a choir

of black gulls squawks, their plainsong meant for him: a welcoming.
        He slides along a quay,
as unobtrusive as a charter boat, a sloop just home from cruising to
        Drake's Bay.

vi

Quark. Least particle. Most matterless. Nothing known resists your
        passing through:
a summer spent at sea, a storm survived. And of the things he carries
        home, a few

now haunt his looks, his face appearing hard along the jawline, and
        behind his eyes
a presence that his mother takes for tears. She's seen it, too, a cen-
        trifuge that lies

just below the skin, which, once it's known, unhinges our percep-
        tion, like a blade
that shows the student his first open heart. Afterward, in his room,
        the scene's replayed:

from glassy seas, smoke rises vertically. In fresher breezes, breaking
        heaps and spray.
In strong gale force, high waves, spindrift off crests, then whitened
        streaky foam. Force nine all day.

From seven-meter waves, the *Mermaid* drops down troughs as deep
        as she is long. How small
he has become, like sea wrack or a reed. A single note, a broken
        string, a call:

the sounds his mouth contains. He cries aloud, hearing his voice
        diminished in the waves,
and, though he's kept on course, his mind's too tired to fathom all
        that's left or count the days.

NOSTALGIA FOR A NEW CITY

i

Sun-going, seaside grid, your dozen fogbound cargo ships
zip up the jade Gate, homeward, where tide is leaving, flowing.

ii

Tourist garden implies us. Carp trawl on tanbark mirrors
clearer than oolong we drain for its cut leaves, you insist.

iii

Dark. Across the J, leather pants end in newsprint. Half-hid,
a kid on cement steps listens to the ticking of sparks.

INVENTION WITH SEASCAPE

Let's say our days were not immutable
but free for us to order as we choose.
Arrayed at noon, our possibilities

would hang like summer linens airing dry,
blown front- or sidewise in the saltish air,
simultaneous, available.

The prospect of our seaside lands would sprawl,
as: item, one fen; item, one ravine;
one snatch of orchard bruised with ripening fruit.

Still, at the horizon, what sudden wind
gathers now to dash this fantasy
in swells from distant waters drawing close:

a rack of breakers blanketed in smoke,
rolling, consequential, a travesty
of our wish to stipulate or fend them off?

ORACLE OF THE GREAT OAK

Forget your question a while.
                              First, turn and see
the roadway threading squares of winter wheat,
fences bound with scrub. Take in the town,
its rooftops like masterstrokes of royal blue.
And notice, too, the crazed geometry
of broken cornstalks bristling the hills,
how balanced perfectly beneath a wisp
of cumulus they jut in freezing gray.
This equipoise comes rarely, as you know.
I don't say *never*. I myself have felt
such calm before, though seldom:
                              As a child,
I woke in sunlight on my parents' berth
aboard a packet moored in a fjord.
The hush beneath its glowering cliffs spread out
like palms laid on an altar, and the sea
along the Norwegian coast, as cold as death,
shone dazzling, benign. That was the first.
Then later at the University
of Freiburg, as a young man I heard bells
at a garret window mix with water-sound
careering through the streets in ancient troths.
The markets smelled of coffee and spilt beer.
Strange what one remembers, stranger still
to think how these oases of rapt thought
could lead one here.

How have I come this way?
I hardly know. Nor can I tell you why
I chose to stay, or how then I became
the voice of this arthritic tree, though not
its sayings' source. It couldn't matter less.
My gift is, well, hardly a gift at all,
like speaking different languages from birth.
I've learned that I am home, that I'll be buried
beside this fist of roots. Not long from now.
In the meantime, travelers find their way to me,
each harboring his query for these boughs.
With gifts and food they leave, I have enough.
Who would disturb this peace?
                            Our end is known.
This great oak speaks through me, the tranced-out ape
of its thoughts, the medium, if you will, through which
the sound of leaves coheres in speech. The rest:
a rustling resolved into, not reason,
but darker figures suited to our fates.
There's the message, there's the tree, and there is I.
Mostly, the branches thrash like metal grates,
a shivaree to toast the marriage bed
grinding down to groans of factories,
or a rustling of innumerable books—
their pages safe from Alexandrian fires
or the dozing aesthete's fumbled cigarette—
conveying their immortal, hidden will
that no one, not the god himself, controls.
I've seen the faithful crumble with the weight
of knowing what befalls our brittle lives.
You're having second thoughts?
                                 Well. It is late.
In truth, it's better not to ask, I've found;

the news is never good, and it infects
the seeker with a plague that courses through him
until he's pure contagion. Yet they come,
and leave much as you will, though blinder than
when they arrived. A sickness eats their eyes.
Below, you'll find a hotel on the square.
Just say you met me here; no need for names.
Tell them you climbed the hill and that we spoke,
that in the morning you will start for home.
Goodnight. How fortunate: You see the moon
that leads you on the path and me to bed?

GRACIE PIER

The way, in painting, an abandoned shack
    Dwarfed beneath a common stand
Of elm trees lends proportion to the scene,
A man beside the dock suggests its size.

Before he paused, no one had stopped for hours
    To wonder at this monkey puzzle
Of timber torn from iron lashed on piles,
In splinters like a chaise of cracked rattan.

A length of chain-link hangs between the walk
    And river-sloping planks now black
From fires set by someone, likely kids,
When uptown ferries fell into disuse.

But what does fencing here mean to protect?
    Not property from vandalism,
Since all attempts to save the value failed
Before these razored spools were tacked in place.

More likely it's to keep ourselves from harm,
    So twilit couples coming here
To cool the rush of love in dampened air
Will not misstep and come to in the tide;

Or, in despair, this man, still loitering,
    Won't sate an impulse to be gone

And drop into the water soundlessly,
But must remain outside his utter ruin,

Put off by metal from a last rash act.
        Though that's not why he's come today,
He thinks, before he sets his walking stick
And finds the path awash in floods of joggers.

The brackish eddies stretching east to Queens
        Keep spiraling behind his eyes
Until he finds the downturn toward the street.
Still weighing what that wooden folly posed,

He makes his way crosstown, just as the sun
        Dips below the waterline
Of buildings on the Yorkville avenues,
And all remaining signs of him are gone.

THE DOUBLE

On Sheep Meadow an old man picks his way
past sunning bodies, which, though it's early April,
fill the grass. The wind lifts up his coattails—
flings them sidelong, flapping against his cane—
     in the distance.

And as he comes across the wide expanse
of green he seems to float over blowing shoals,
walking on the risen Styx, and hunched,
for old men tire easily (he is tired)
      on windy passages.

But wind has power to blur the wobbly world:
a tall man certainly, but hardly old—
my age, in fact. How had there been a cane?
Unless the brain works with the eye to fill in
      for gaps we find.

Now close, he looks like me. Strange to think
that he's no nearer age and death than I,
the young man walking out of the older man
like a snake skin shed, the same one he will wear
      again someday.

NOTES

The Graven Image
The *New York Observer* article from which the epigraph is taken was written by Mark Lasswell. While the words of the epigraph are Mr. Lasswell's, I have taken liberties with the order of the phrases, using ellipses to help to indicate this re-arrangement.

Sad Is Eros, Builder of Cities
My thanks to Alfred Corn for suggesting the title of this poem, which is taken from W. H. Auden's "In Memory of Sigmund Freud."

Upon Julia's Breasts
This poem is the result of a commission from George Plimpton and the editors of the *Paris Review*, who provided the title and asked for a poem. The title of Robert Herrick's great poem was chosen from a list that ranged from film titles (*Jaws, Dr. Strangelove*) to the fanciful ("An Empty Surfboard on a Still Sea").

His Boat
The italic passages that appear in section iii are paraphrases of Japanese haiku translated by Harry Behn in *Cricket Songs* (New York: Harcourt, Brace & World, 1964, pages 1 and 6). The first is by Onitsura, the second by Buson.

Oracle of the Great Oak
This poem was suggested by a talk on oracles given by Michael Wood at the New York Institute for the Humanities at NYU. Any rough handling of the material is entirely my own doing.

ABOUT THE AUTHOR

David Yezzi is the director of New York's 92nd Street Y Unterberg Poetry Center. His critical writings have been published in the *New York Times, New Yorker,* and other major publications. His poetry has appeared in *New Republic, Paris Review, Yale Review, New England Review,* and *New Criterion,* among other journals. This is his first book of poetry.